2012

CORALS

HERBERT S. ZIM

illustrated by René Martin

William Morrow and Company
New York 1966

№ 2 0 1 7 /

Fourth printing, November 1970

The author thanks Dr. Robert E. Schroeder, of the Department of Bi-
ology, University of Miami, and Dr. Frederick M. Bayer, of the Insti-
tute of Marine Science, University of Miami, for reviewing the manu-
script and for supplying specimens and helpful criticisms of the art.

Excepting man, builder of roads, dams, and cities, no animals have altered the face of the earth as much as the small, weak-bodied corals. These simple creatures, aided by related animals and by several kinds of seaweeds, have built thousands of miles of reefs on which hundreds of islands have formed.

Millions of acres of land, mainly in the Pacific and Indian Oceans and some in the Atlantic, are there because of what coral animals have done.

In widely separated places limestone rocks make up an important part of the land. Many of these limestone deposits were formed millions of years ago largely or entirely from corals. In the Alps rock layers over half a mile thick are composed mainly of coral limestone. In other sections of Europe and America coral rocks extend for miles. The famous Capitan Reef formed by primitive corals, in Texas some 250 million years ago, is 1200 feet thick and 400 miles long.

Coral limestones are common in the Alps.

Wherever coral rocks and coral reefs are found, they prove that the land was once under the sea. Coral reefs, 4000 feet above the sea, on mountainsides in Timor show how great past changes have been on this Malaysian island.

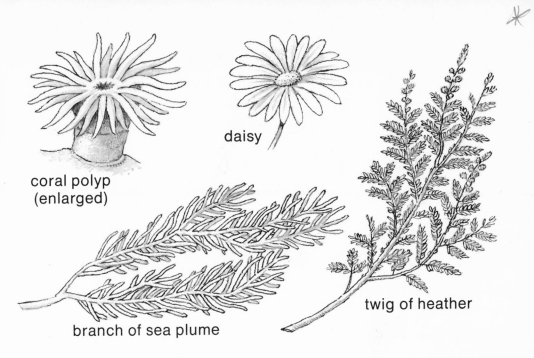

coral polyp
(enlarged)

daisy

branch of sea plume

twig of heather

Living corals look so unlike most other creatures that only about 200 years ago scientists finally agreed they were not plants but animals. Single coral animals and some of the colonies of coral look like flowering plants. But the way their bodies are built and the way they live, feed, and grow, mark corals as simple animals related to jellyfish and sea anemones.

The word *coral* (which comes from Latin) is used for both the animal and the stony "skeleton" that it builds. It is a word that makes us think of the great reefs that rise in tropical seas—and there most corals live.

But there are other kinds of corals too. In total nearly 5000 species are known. Some close relatives of the reef-building corals live in the deep sea, at depths up to three miles. Most of these deep-sea corals are also found in shallower water, from 500 to 1500 feet deep, where some form reefs. They live in much colder water than the reef-building corals. Some survive where the water is close to freezing. Most grow best, however, in water between 40 to 50 degrees Fahrenheit.

depth
¼ to 3
miles

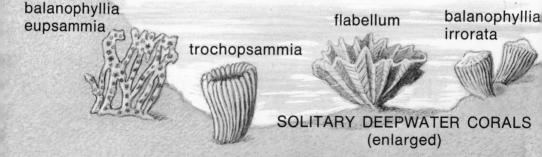

balanophyllia
eupsammia

trochopsammia

flabellum

balanophyllia
irrorata

SOLITARY DEEPWATER CORALS
(enlarged)

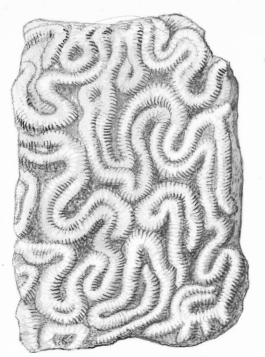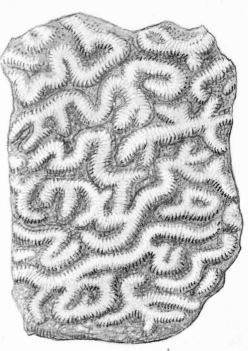

fossil diploria coral
about 100 million years old

modern diploria coral
(West Indies)

Reef-building corals first appeared about 200 million years ago. In the 100 million years that followed most of the families that are still living today were established. Fossil reef corals, found in rocks that are only 10 to 50 million years old, look very much like the kinds that exist now.

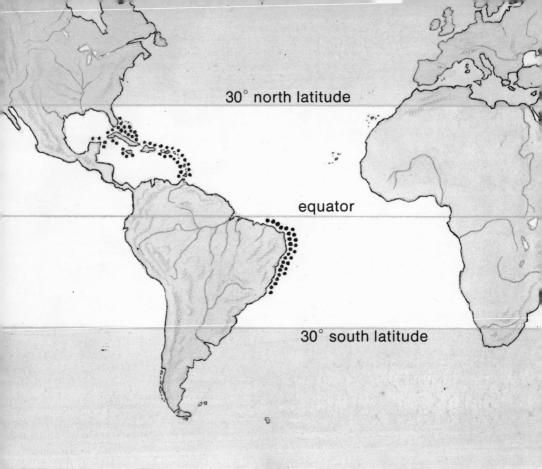

Reef corals grow best in clear ocean water. Four factors control their growth: the temperature of the water, the amount of salt in it, the amount of light that reaches the coral animals, and the supply of food.

Most reef corals thrive in water whose tem-

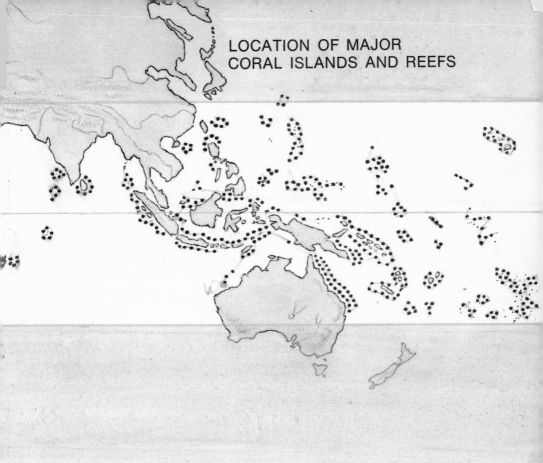

perature stays between 77 and 85 degrees Fahrenheit. They can live at temperatures as low as 60 degrees, but will not grow to form large colonies. This need for warm water places most of the reef corals in a belt about 30 degrees wide on either side of the equator.

Yet when the water temperature gets as high as 96 degrees, as it does in tropical shallows, the coral animals die.

On the western edge of the great continents, the ocean currents often flow from colder regions or from greater depths. Hence, the surface temperature is lowered. Coral reefs are, therefore, absent on the western coasts of North and South America, Africa, and Australia. On the eastern coasts, which are usually warmed by currents moving north or south from the equator, coral reefs are often found. Along the Florida Keys in the Atlantic, there

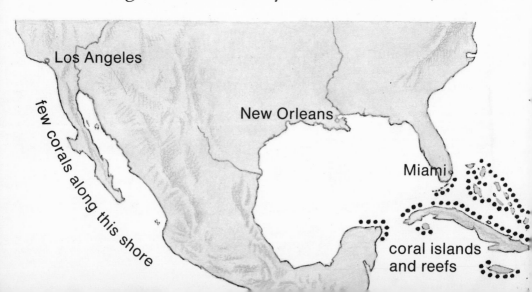

Los Angeles

few corals along this shore

New Orleans

Miami

coral islands and reefs

is a large one close to the Gulf Stream. But off Lower California, at the same latitude (25 degrees north), there are none because the water is much colder.

In places like some bays and gulfs the circulation of seawater is cut down. The amount of salt in the water becomes distinctly higher than the amount in the open seas, and corals will not grow there. They also cannot live near the mouth of rivers where there is too little salt in the water. Reef-building corals do best when the salt content in the sea is about average—three and one-half percent.

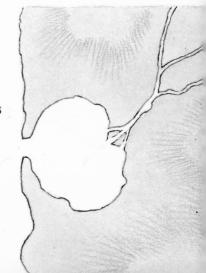

At left, in landlocked bay, evaporation makes seawater more salty.

At right, river dilutes water in bay making it less salty.

The great difference between plants and animals is that plants can use sunlight to manufacture their own food while animals cannot. Sooner or later all animals must get their food from plants. For this reason, animals do not need sunlight. Why should coral animals be an exception? We can find the answer only by looking at a tiny coral animal under a microscope. Imbedded under the "skin" of the coral animals are very small one-celled plants. They are a kind of simple algae, which actually live in the coral animals. Because of them, the corals need light.

algae cells

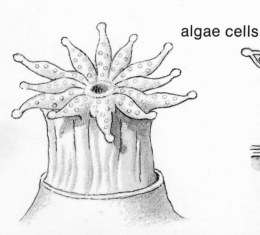

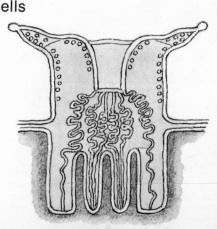

polyp
(enlarged 10 times)

vertical section

The single coral animal, called a polyp, is soft and small. Some coral polyps can live without algae. Normally both corals and algae live together and probably both benefit from so doing. But exactly how is still an unanswered question. Polyps feed only on other small animals, which they quickly digest. The algae may use the waste of the polyps as a kind of fertilizer. The polyps, in turn, may use the oxygen given off by the algae in sunlight. However, the polyps do not use the algae in their tissues as food.

Besides the algae that live in coral animals

Giant clams of the Australian reefs have fleshy folds in which thousands of algae live.

and in some of the large clams, there often are many kinds and large numbers of free-living algae in a coral reef. This observation led one expert to point out that, at times, an entire coral reef may act more like a plant than an animal. In bright sunlight a coral reef may release surplus oxygen into the sea as a huge bed of seaweed does.

The need for both light and warmth limits the range of reef corals to shallow water, usually no deeper than 150 feet, though occasionally corals live as deep as 250 feet. Coral reefs are awash at low tide, and the best growths are found from just below the low-tide mark to a depth of 50 or 60 feet.

The coral animals that create reefs and islands are very simple. All corals belong in the same large group (phylum) as jellyfish,

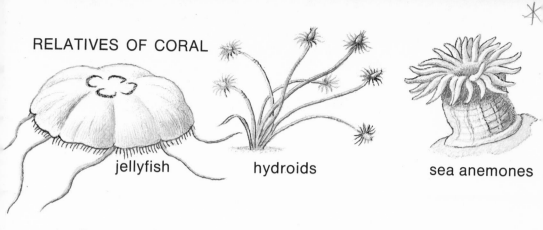

RELATIVES OF CORAL

jellyfish   hydroids   sea anemones

hydras, and many other soft-bodied animals. All live in water and most have stinging cells that help them capture food. The typical coral animal is something like a soft rubber ball punched in on one side. The inside of the cuplike hollow forms the central cavity. Around the top of the cup is a ring of small arms, or tentacles.

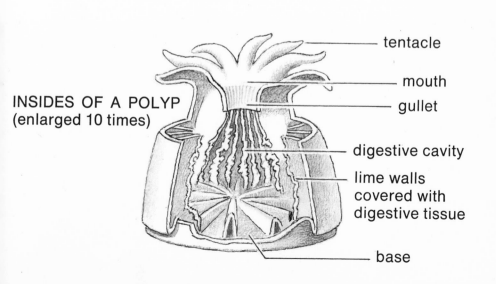

INSIDES OF A POLYP
(enlarged 10 times)

tentacle

mouth

gullet

digestive cavity

lime walls
covered with
digestive tissue

base

The reef-building corals, also called stony corals or madrepore corals, belong in a subgroup with the sea anemones. Members of this group always have six tentacles or a multiple of six—such as 12, 18, and 24—around their mouth. The sea anemones live singly or in small clumps. A few reef corals live singly, but most form large colonies with thousands upon thousands of polyps.

Another feature of the six-tentacle group is that the edge of the mouth just inside the ring of tentacles turns in and forms a gullet connecting to the central cavity. The cavity walls are folded vertically, and each fold fits into a groove in the coral cup that surrounds the polyp. The vertical folds greatly increase the area of the cavity walls, and so speed up the digestion of food.

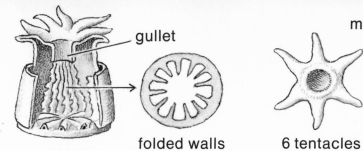

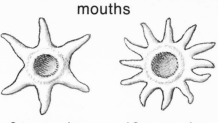

gullet

folded walls

mouths

6 tentacles

12 tentacles

When a coral animal is feeding, the tentacles wave in all directions and trap tiny floating plankton animals, small shrimp, or even tiny fish. The captured animal, often killed by the stinging cells in the tentacles, is pushed down the gullet into the central cavity, where it is digested.

The soft corals make up another group, which includes sea pens, sea plumes, sea fans, and organ-pipe coral. Soft corals sport eight feathery tentacles around each polyp mouth.

SOFT CORALS

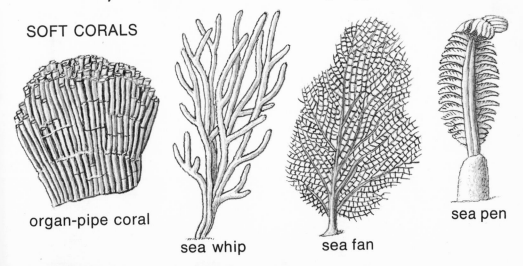

organ-pipe coral

sea whip

sea fan

sea pen

star coral
single polyps

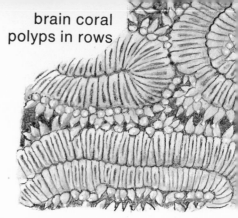

brain coral
polyps in rows

The bit of white coral skeleton that a vacationer brings back as a souvenir of his Southern vacation gives one little idea of what living coral is like. It also may be difficult to identify. About 2500 different kinds, or species, of madrepore corals have been named. Only a few kinds are easy to recognize. The others need careful study. There are also over 2000 kinds of soft corals.

Polyps of colonial reef corals are small—from pinhead size to one quarter or one half of an inch. Each polyp in a colonial coral may live in a separate cup. Sometimes the cups run together to form a row or a ridge. Each polyp or row of polyps secretes lime, building up the walls of the "skeleton" around it. The cups or rows have distinct patterns, which aid identification of different corals.

The cells that form the outer layer of the polyp (except on the tentacles) are able to extract the lime that is dissolved in seawater. Dissolved in 1000 pounds of seawater (about 125 gallons) are 1.4 pounds of lime, 27.2 pounds of table salt, and many other chemicals. The living coral cells extract the lime, combine it with carbon dioxide and make the mineral aragonite—a form of calcium

The seas contain about 300 million cubic miles of water. Each cubic mile contains about 170 million pounds of chemicals including:

Sodium chloride	130 million pounds
Magnesium chloride	18
Magnesium sulfate	9
Calcium sulfate	6
Potassium sulfate	4
Calcium carbonate	0.6
Magnesium bromide	0.4

and many more in smaller amounts.

carbonate containing calcium (lime) plus carbon and oxygen. Aragonite is also formed in other ways, but the tiny polyps make millions upon millions of tons. The mineral formed this way, the rock made of it, and the animal that makes it are all called coral.

The coral polyp grows attached to the bottom of its coral cup. As long as it is alive and growing, it keeps building the walls and bottom of the cup making the coral "skeleton" larger and heavier each year. The polyp itself forms "buds" or it divides in two. Either way, new polyps appear and increase the size of the colony.

polyp dividing

polyp budding

The soft polyps with their waving tentacles are not often seen. They remain shut or partly shut by day and open only at night when they feed. If illuminated then, the breathtaking colors—pinks, reds, purples, yellows, greens, and golden browns—of the open polyps become visible.

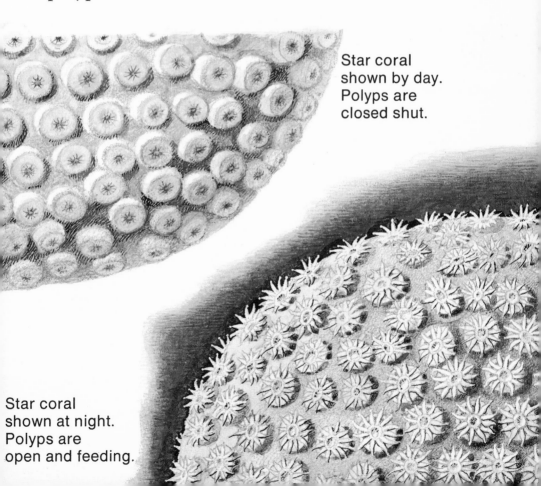

Star coral shown by day. Polyps are closed shut.

Star coral shown at night. Polyps are open and feeding.

Coral polyps also develop from the sperm and egg cells of mature polyps, which float in the water. A fertilized egg begins to grow as it floats, but it must settle on a hard, rough bottom. If it drifts into mud or silt, it dies. When an egg lands on rock, it anchors and begins to grow. The polyp gets larger. By budding and dividing it may become a whole new colony. In that way a new reef gets started or an old one spreads.

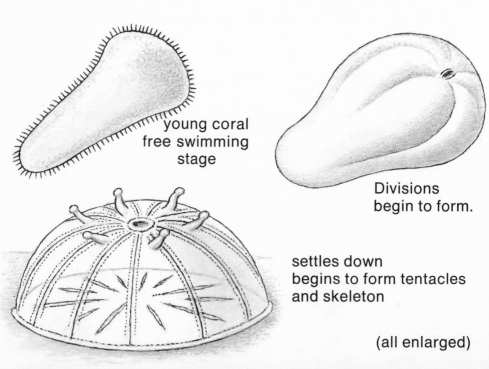

young coral
free swimming
stage

Divisions
begin to form.

settles down
begins to form tentacles
and skeleton

(all enlarged)

living coral, covered at high tide

growing

edge

coral boulder

dead coral

A CORAL PLATFORM

Reef corals grow best when there is a constant movement of the water around them. Moving water in the open ocean contains more oxygen and usually very little mud and silt. It also brings a supply of tiny plants and animals (plankton) over the coral reef. Coral animals, feeding on the tiny floating animals of the sea, are just as much flesh eaters as sharks or tigers.

GROWTH OF CORAL IN ONE YEAR
(volume increase)

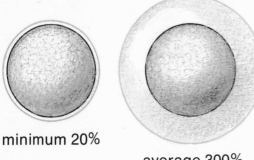

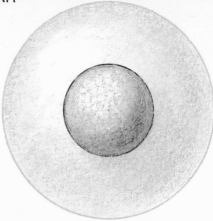

minimum 20%

average 300%

maximum 1200%

When conditions are right, billions of tiny coral animals grow and, in the process, build up coral—and coral makes the reef. The rate of growth depends on the kind of coral. Some kinds of polyps produce a heavy, dense coral "skeleton" and hence grow more slowly. Measured samples in the Pacific Ocean increased in weight at least 20 percent a year. Most kinds grew more rapidly. The light, porous corals may increase in weight as much as 1200 percent—one pound of coral becoming

LENGTH OF BRANCHES
(growth in one year)

from 1/10 of an inch

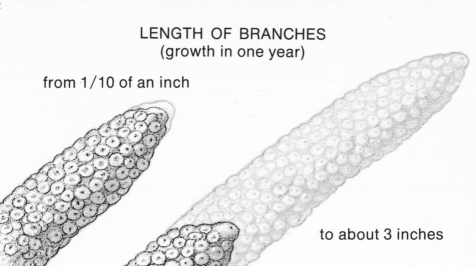

to about 3 inches

13 pounds in one year. On an average, coral colonies increase in weight about 300 percent a year. A sample branch of coral may lengthen from one tenth of an inch to as much as three inches in a year. In Florida reefs, coral branches may increase in diameter from one half to two inches annually. Each type of coral has its own pattern of growth. Here are some well-known corals. You can probably identify specimens you get by comparing them with the pictures.

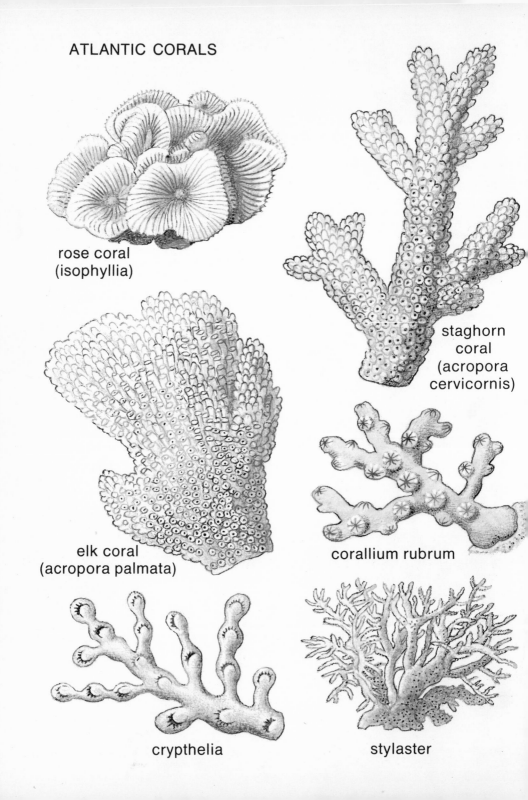

ATLANTIC CORALS

rose coral
(isophyllia)

staghorn
coral
(acropora
cervicornis)

elk coral
(acropora palmata)

corallium rubrum

crypthelia

stylaster

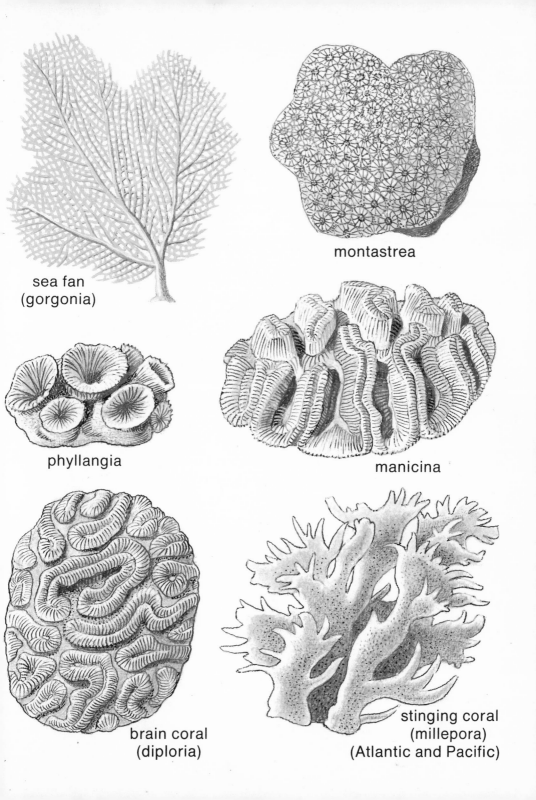

sea fan
(gorgonia)

montastrea

phyllangia

manicina

brain coral
(diploria)

stinging coral
(millepora)
(Atlantic and Pacific)

In some coral reefs of Florida and the Caribbean, less than a dozen kinds of corals may be growing. In some Pacific reefs, as many as three dozen or more kinds may live together. These coral colonies with dozens of other plants and animals make up the reef.

PACIFIC CORALS

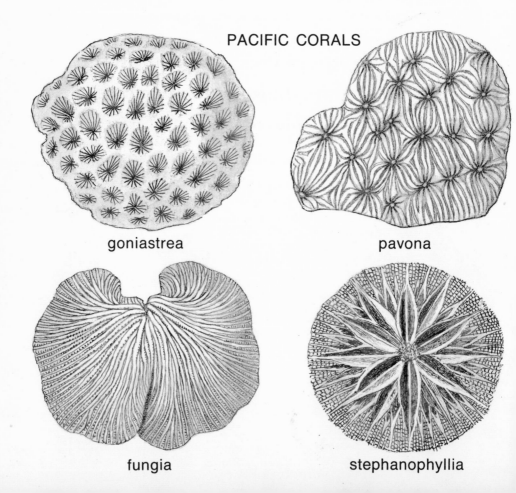

goniastrea

pavona

fungia

stephanophyllia

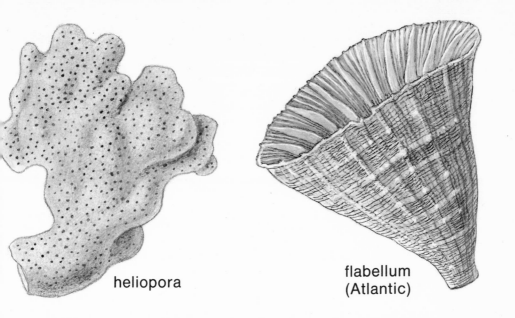

heliopora

flabellum
(Atlantic)

Many corals form lines of growth that are something like the rings in a tree trunk. See them in the drawing of flabellum above. It may be possible to measure the daily, monthly, and yearly growth of living corals and of fossil corals millions of years old. The study of fossil corals seems to suggest that the year is slowly getting shorter. Corals may soon become very important in the research on the earth's long past.

Coral reefs are not all alike. There are several kinds. Fringing reefs, the most common and widespread, form along rocky shores or around islands. The coral begins to grow just below the low-tide mark and extends outward as a shallow platform. The width of a fringing reef depends on how steeply the underwater shore slopes. A shallow slope helps to make a wide reef. A steep slope makes a narrow one.

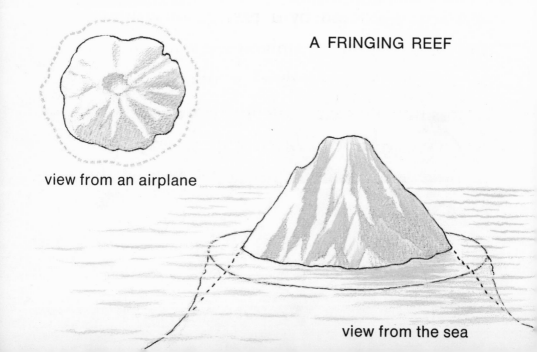

A FRINGING REEF

view from an airplane

view from the sea

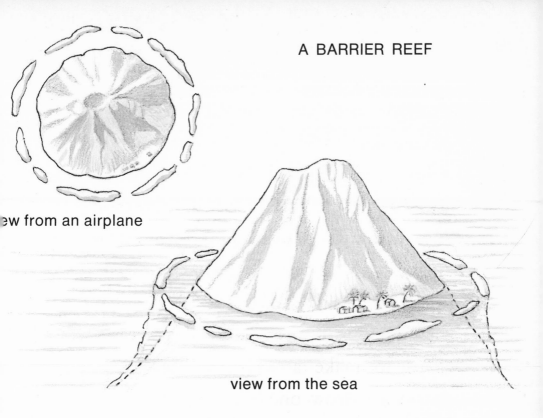

A BARRIER REEF

view from an airplane

view from the sea

Barrier reefs, a second type, are separated from the mainland by a passage or channel. The reef may be mainly underwater, as in parts of the West Indies, or it may include chains of islands, as in the Great Barrier Reef of Australia. The channel between the reef and the mainland may narrow down to less than a mile, or it may be much wider.

The channel separating the Great Barrier Reef from the mainland is 15 to 70 miles wide. This giant reef, 1200 miles long, covers about 80,000 square miles—an area about the size of South Dakota. Only ten major passages lead through the reef into the open ocean, so the island areas along the reef channel are difficult to reach.

The bank reefs off the Florida Keys and in the Bahamas resemble barrier reefs, but also differ from them in important ways.

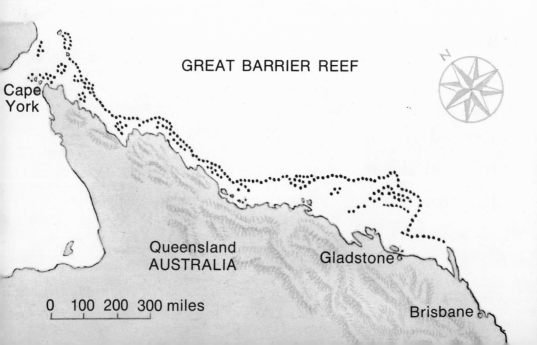

GREAT BARRIER REEF

Cape York

Queensland
AUSTRALIA

Gladstone

Brisbane

0   100 200 300 miles

Best known of the coral reefs are atolls, or coral islands. These ring- or horseshoe-shaped reefs enclose lagoons—quiet, shallow areas of the sea. The lagoon may be only a few yards across, or it may be 10 to 20 miles wide. None is over 180 feet deep, and most are much less than that. Above the living reef are one or more islands where coral sand has piled high enough for trees to grow. People live on these low atolls, which are safe, except during typhoons or other severe storms.

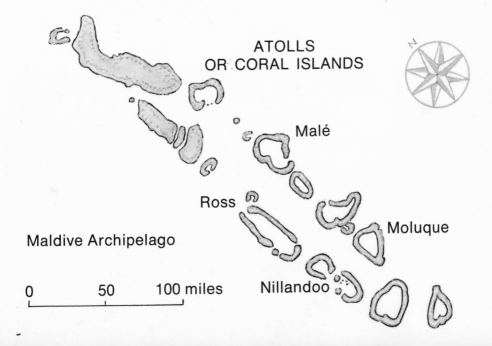

ATOLLS
OR CORAL ISLANDS

Malé

Ross

Moluque

Maldive Archipelago

Nillandoo

0   50   100 miles

Europeans who explored tropic seas, especially the South Pacific from the 1600's to the 1800's, were astonished by the doughnut-shaped atolls and other coral formations. First the sailors and explorers, later the scientists, described the coral reefs and the many kinds of coral in them. New species of fishes, crabs, and smaller sea animals were discovered in the lagoons and in the open sea. Because their ships were wrecked on them, sailors feared the reefs. Great Britain and other seafaring nations sent naval ships to locate, chart, and mark the reefs and atolls. But no one offered a good explanation as to how the reefs and atolls had formed.

Charles Darwin made his famous round-the-world voyage on the ship *Beagle*, from 1831 to 1836. He recorded thousands of observations in his notebooks, which we can read today. Darwin described the three kinds of reefs he studied in the Pacific: fringing, barrier, and atoll. He observed that many small volcanic islands in the Pacific rose from the water in cone-shaped peaks. These islands were usually surrounded by a fringing coral reef that formed a shallow platform. Using all these facts, after he returned to England, Darwin developed his theory of how coral reefs formed.

If a volcanic island were to sink very slowly, due to earth movements, the fringing coral reef would begin to grow faster at its outer fringe. There the moving shallow water is fresh and rich in oxygen. After thousands of years of settling, only the tip of the island mountain remains above the water. But the fast-growing coral, in the meantime, has formed a complete ring around the volcanic cone, with a lagoon separating the reef from

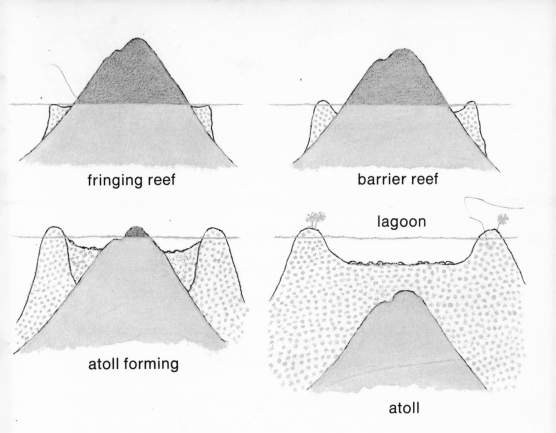

fringing reef

barrier reef

atoll forming

lagoon

atoll

the mountain. Darwin saw such islands with barrier reefs making a circle around them.

With passing time, as the island continues to sink the mountain peak gradually disappears. Only the circle of coral with a lagoon at its center remains and continues to grow. Dead coral, broken by waves, fills the lagoon

atoll from air

so that it stays shallow. Thus an atoll is formed. And, as centuries go by, broken coral is ground into sand. Winds carry the sand up from the beach to form dunes. There plants take root and roots anchor the sand. The atoll becomes a permanent island.

Probing farther into atolls and lagoons, scientists have made some important discoveries. Holes bored into several lagoons showed that coral sand and debris go down a thousand feet or more. At Bikini Atoll, measurements showed that the coral was at least 1800 feet thick and that the hard volcanic rock was over a mile down. Drill holes at Eniwetok Atoll went down through 4000 feet of coral before volcanic rock was reached. These findings can only mean that earth movements and changes in sea level have been very great.

We now know that the changes in ocean level are usually due to changes in climate. When the climate has become colder, over thousands of years, huge glaciers or ice sheets have formed. At least four times in the past million years such continental glaciers have covered much of the Northern Hemisphere with ice sheets up to a mile thick.

1000 feet

2000 feet

coral rock

3000 feet

4000 feet

volcanic platform

Glaciers form when the winter snow is so thick that all of it does not melt during the warm summer. When cold weather comes again, some of last winter's snow still remains. By then it has hardened into ice, and the thickness of the ice layer increases year after year. As the ice grows thicker less water flows each summer from melting glaciers. Water that would normally flow back into the sea remains landlocked in the ice. As a result, the level of the oceans begins to drop slowly year after year.

The giant ice sheets that once covered much of Europe and North America locked up enough water to cause a 300-foot drop in the oceans. Stretches of land that had been underwater were exposed. So were coral reefs and atolls. The sea level went down slowly, much less than an inch a year, but after a

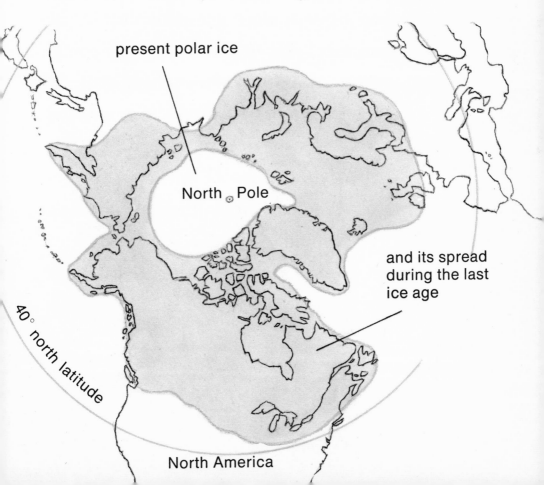

present polar ice

North Pole

and its spread during the last ice age

40° north latitude

North America

while reefs were exposed even at high tide. Then wind, rain, waves, and currents wore them down till they were back to sea level. New fringing reefs grew on the edges of the old worn-down reefs. Later the air slowly warmed, more ice melted, and the seas began to rise. Corals grew upward in the rising seas, and the reefs spread outward.

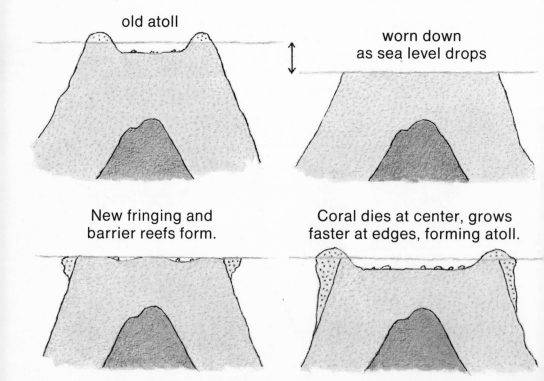

old atoll

worn down
as sea level drops

New fringing and
barrier reefs form.

Coral dies at center, grows
faster at edges, forming atoll.

As thousands of years passed, these changing conditions slowly turned fringing reefs into barrier reefs, and barrier reefs into atolls.

In the Florida Keys and parts of the West Indies, reefs probably formed on different types of platforms. Therefore, they did not develop in the same way as those in the South Pacific. There are, for example, few true atolls in the Caribbean area.

The story of how coral reefs are formed is not yet fully understood in all its details. In years ahead much more will be learned.

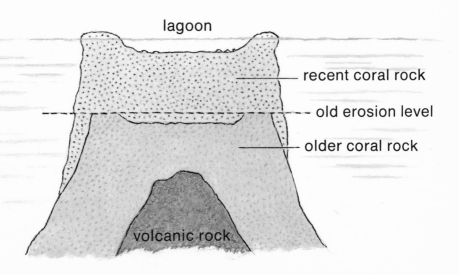

lagoon
recent coral rock
old erosion level
older coral rock
volcanic rock

The growth of a coral reef, like the growth of all living things, is a balance between building up and tearing down. From its beginning, a reef suffers from the battering of waves and currents. Sometimes land rises slowly and the reef appears above water. This exposure kills the coral. Parts of a large reef grow while other parts die. As the battering of the sea continues, branches of coral are broken off and ground into sand that fills part of the lagoon. Sand may form coral beaches, if the ocean currents permit. Sometimes the coral sand and larger fragments of coral are cemented together into a kind of coral rock. Pockets and hollows in the rock catch and hold rain water. The trade winds mold the sand into dunes. Coconuts, mangroves, sea grapes, and other seashore plants take root. They hold the sand and begin

mangrove

sea grape

to form soil. People come and a settlement begins. In the meantime, the true coral reef growing and spreading below the tidemark is alive and full of activity.

To see a coral reef closely, one must get into the water or under its surface. A glass-bottomed bucket or glass-bottomed boat reveals some of the wonders of a reef—but such views are like looking into a room through a key-hole. One must enter the reef underwater to see it completely.

Nowhere in the world is a coral reef as easy to see as in the Florida Keys, much of which are reefs formed about 100,000 years ago. The reef begins off Cape Florida, near Miami, and parallels the islands for some two hundred miles. Similar reefs are found in the Bahamas to the east and all through the West Indies.

Off Key Largo a section of the reef, covering about 75 square miles, has been set aside as the first underwater park in the United States. There on calm days visitors can see the world of the coral reef for themselves. First and most obvious are the corals. Branching angular staghorn corals catch the eye immediately. Nearby grow rounded brain corals, their surface like a jigsaw puzzle. Stinging corals, different from the reef-building kinds, form a brownish crust over the dead madrepore species.

Miami

KEY LARGO

Coral Reef Park

Key West

0 10 20 30 40 50
statute miles

3862 F

Equally beautiful and even more exciting are the sea plumes and sea fans. These colonies of soft corals build a horny "skeleton" that twists back and forth with the waves and currents. Almost everywhere are colorful patches of encrusting corals, which cover the older parts of the reef corals.

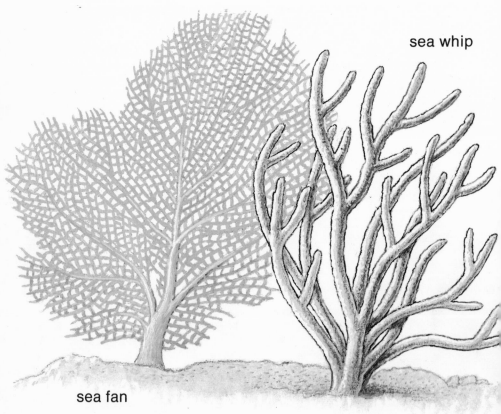

sea whip

sea fan

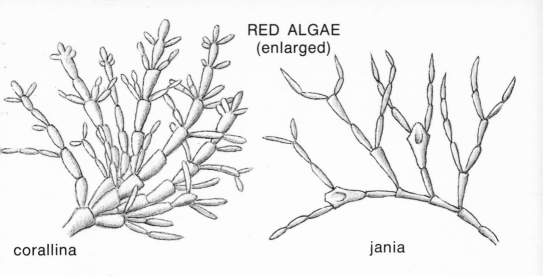

RED ALGAE
(enlarged)

corallina

jania

Near the surface and in the quiet parts of the reef are great tangled patches of red coraline algae. These plants also take lime from the sea and add a great deal of it to the reef area. On a smaller scale, several kinds of marine green algae do the same thing.

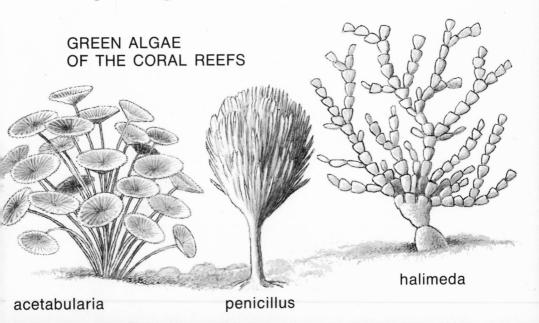

GREEN ALGAE
OF THE CORAL REEFS

acetabularia

penicillus

halimeda

The Florida reef consists of many kinds of living things, forming a tight community. The animals are most abundant. In addition to the corals, hundreds of kinds of other animals with and without backbones add to the reef's population. Among them are some of the most beautiful and bizarre of all fishes.

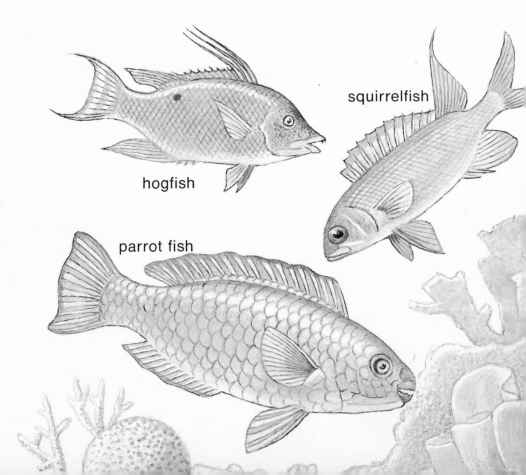

hogfish

squirrelfish

parrot fish

Scores of small animals work actively on the reef. Some worms, snails, and other animals secrete lime, building up the reef. Similar animals bore into the coral and help break it down. Sponges, mollusks, tube worms, and sea urchins work in this way. Several kinds of parrot fish crush the dead coral with their heavy grinding teeth and feed on the algae growing on them. Other animals that are part of the reef community—starfish, sea cucumbers, and many kinds of shrimp and crabs—go their way without affecting the coral itself.

porkfish

grouper

The plants and animals, such as the coral tube worm and red algae, that grow fixed in one place make up the bulk of the reef. Other animals, like mollusks and sea urchins, move around in limited ways. These colorful attached plants and animals are the part of the reef that catches one's eye. Beautiful as they are, the reef would be much less of a wonderland if it were not for the many kinds of fish that live in and around the corals. Reef fishes are usually small, though some groupers may weigh hundreds of pounds. The sharks and barracudas are large too, but they patrol the edges of the reef and do not really live as part of it.

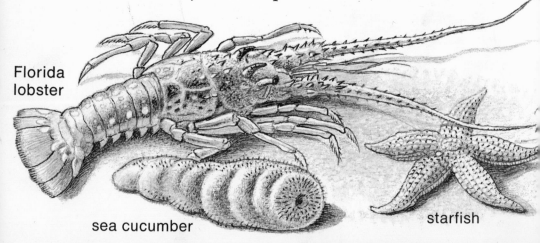

Florida lobster

sea cucumber

starfish

As striking as any of the colorful animals on the reef are the angelfish. These fairly large, flattened fish may be jet black, black speckled with yellow, or brilliant blue with red, orange, and yellow on the fins and tail. Somewhat like them, with equally bold patterns, are the butterfly fish.

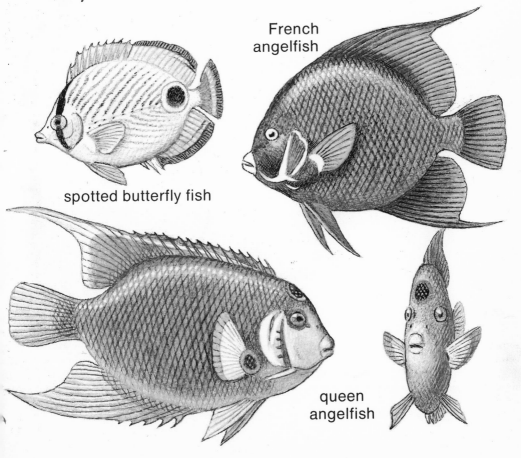

French angelfish

spotted butterfly fish

queen angelfish

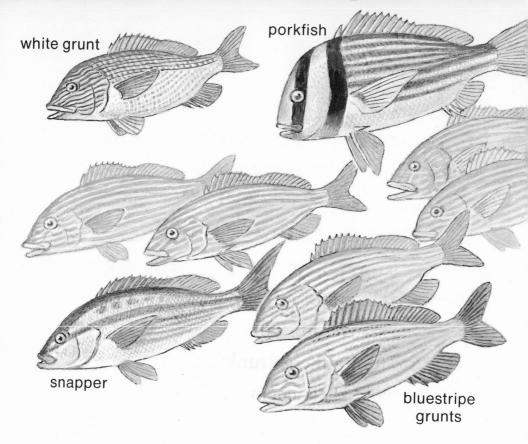

white grunt
porkfish
snapper
bluestripe grunts

Grunts are the most plentiful fish on the reef. Schools of them sweep by, hundreds at a time, in and around the coral. Among the most handsome of the grunts are the porkfish and the bluestripe. Young snappers also abound in the reef and sometimes swim with the grunts. Larger kinds of snappers prefer deeper water.

Green moray eels hide in crevices and lash out to grab nearby prey. Several kinds of wrasses, spadefishes, lookdowns, silvery anchovies, and other smaller fry travel in schools along the reef. One group of fishes on this Florida reef have special ways to protect themselves. Some are encased in armor or spines. Others are able to puff themselves up. Thus triggerfish, filefish, porcupine fish, puffers, trunkfish, cowfish, and sculpins avoid their enemies.

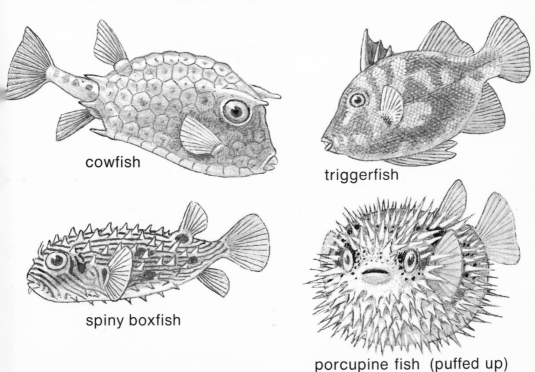

cowfish

triggerfish

spiny boxfish

porcupine fish (puffed up)

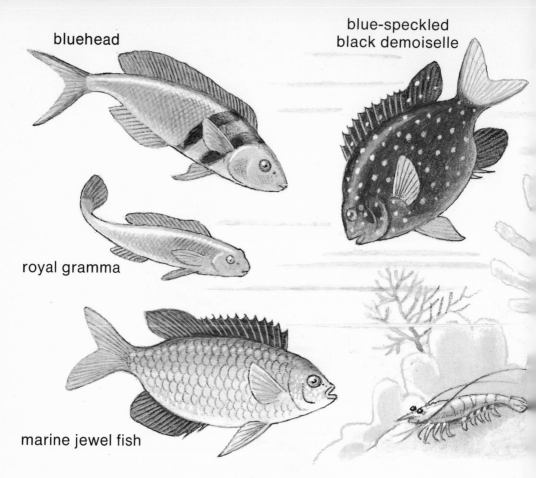

bluehead

blue-speckled
black demoiselle

royal gramma

marine jewel fish

The real beauties of the reef are the smaller reef fishes: the blue-speckled black demoiselle; the royal gramma, a splash of purple and orange; the bluehead, true to its name; the striped sergeant major; and many others. All these fish live together in an ever-changing community, centered on the reef itself.

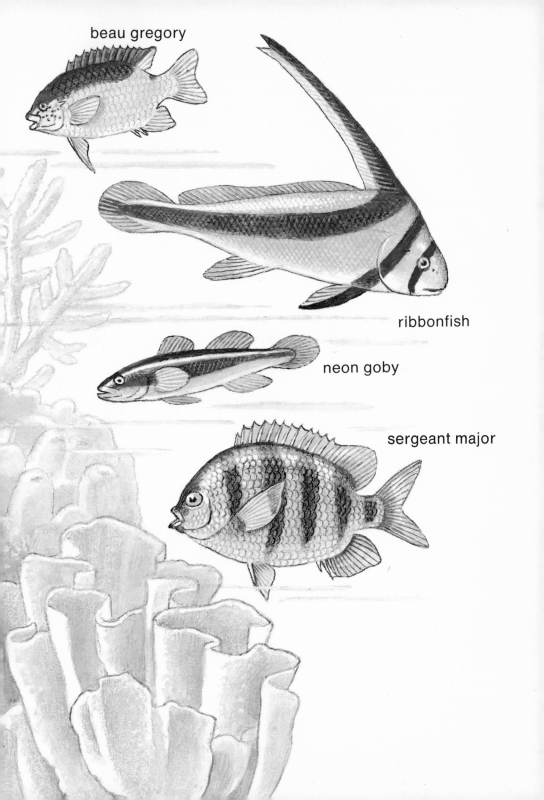

beau gregory

ribbonfish

neon goby

sergeant major

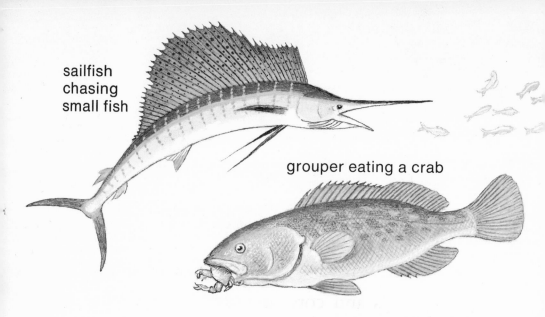

sailfish
chasing
small fish

grouper eating a crab

Larger fishes usually feed on smaller kinds. They, in turn, eat shrimps, worms, and other small marine animals. On the reef there are scores of ways of getting food and scores of ways to keep from being eaten. The reef is both a feeding ground and a hiding place.

The splendor and wonder of the coral reefs come from the many kinds of animal life found in and around them. Almost invisible tube worms may snap open into flowerlike rings of pink or yellow tentacles. Sponges form balls and vases, and cover parts of the reef with an encrusting carpet of red, yellow, or green. The beautiful colors of the underwater reef change with the time of day and the passing clouds.

Automatic lighthouses and buoys mark coral reefs so they are no longer a danger to ships. On the atolls and coral islands of the Pacific and Indian Oceans thousands of people live happily. The sea and their gardens offer them a plentiful food supply. Each year more and more visitors come to coral reefs from Florida to Australia. Many today make an underwater visit to see for themselves what these tiny coral animals can do.

INDEX
Indicates illustration

Algae, 16*, 17*, 18, 53*, 55, 56
Aragonite, 23-24
Atlantic corals, 30*-31*
Atolls, 37*, 38, 40, 41*, 42*, 45, 46*, 47, 63
Balanophyllia, 8*, 9*
Bank reef, 36
Barrier reef, 35*, 36*, 40, 41*, 46*, 47
Bikini Atoll, 42-43
Brain coral (diploria), 22*, 31*, 50
Capitan Reef, 5
Coral Reef Park (Key Largo), 50, 51*
Corallium rubrum, 30*
Crypthelia, 30*
Darwin, Charles, 39-41
Deepwater (deep-sea) corals, 8*, 9*, 10
Desmophyllum, 9*
Elk coral (acropora palmata), 30*
Eniwetok Atoll, 43*
Flabellum, 8*, 33*
Florida Keys, 14, 36, 47, 50, 51*
Florida reef, 32, 54
Food of coral, 21, 27
Fossil (ancient) corals, 10*, 11*, 33
Fringing reef, 34*, 39-40, 41*, 46*, 47
Fungia, 32*
Glaciers, 43, 44*, 45*
Goniastrea, 32*
Great Barrier Reef, 35, 36*
Growth of coral, 28*, 29*

Heliopora, 33*
Hydroid, 19*
Jellyfish, 7, 19*
Lagoon, 37, 38, 40, 41*, 42
Limestone, 5, 23-24
Lophelia, 9*
Madrepora, 9*
Manicina, 31*
Monastrea, 31*
Monomyces, 9*
Organ-pipe, 21*
Pacific corals, 32*
Pavona, 32*
Phyllangia, 31*
Polyp, 7*, 22*, 24*, 25*
    definition, 17
    diagram, 19*
Reef coral (madrepore), 6, 8, 11-15, 14*, 18, 20, 27, 29, 32
Reef fishes, 54*, 55*, 56*, 57*, 58*, 59*, 60*, 61*, 62*
Reproduction of coral, 24, 26
Rose coral (isophyllia), 30*
Sea anemone, 7, 19*, 20
Sea fan (gorgonia), 21*, 31*, 52*
Sea pen, 21*
Sea whip, 21*, 52*
Soft coral, 21*, 25*, 52*
Staghorn coral (acropora cervicornis), 30*
Star coral, 22*, 25*
Stephanophyllia, 32*
Stinging coral (millepora), 31*, 50
Stylaster, 30*
Trochopsammia, 8*, 9*
Tubastraea, 9*